DREAMS LOST IN CHAOS

A COLLECTION OF SHORT POEMS

GABE INGRAM

All these words mean nothing without you.

If only she still dreamt of unicorns,
her life would be so much simpler.

I studied the shape of the tattoo running down
her ribs.

Wanting to run my finger across every line.

If I ever tell you the truth,
you should question every syllable.

We are often most honest in our lies.

Orpheus wasted his time looking back,
I only want to walk forward with you.

I wanted her to reach the stars,
even if all I could do was look at them.

She asked me once,
if she was my muse,
what words could I ever use
if she didn't already know.

I know how it feels to be lost at sea,

It's when I haven't heard from you all day.

Dreams are the gateway to time travel:

Reliving the past....
Exploring infinite futures.

You make me dream of things
I'd forgotten ever existed.

Dreams are wishes
that just haven't come true yet.

The greatest stories
are those that we haven't lived yet.

Holding her face between my hands,
the kisses I placed on her lips
didn't compare to the way my heart
skipped every time she said my name.

She whispered to me her secrets,
and I gave to her my heart.

You're perfect in your imperfections.

Share with me all your secrets,
 so we can create new ones together.

Secrets trickled from her lips,
and I filled my cup with them.

Wanting to drink of her soul.

She weathered every storm,
even when the waves
nearly washed her away.

Talk to me of lost cities,
forgotten dreams,
the meaning of Being.

All the things that matter,
and more importantly,
those that don't.

With each word,
she drew closer to me.

With each look
she pulled further away.

When everything is in chaos,
I think of you and smile.

I'd rather give her dreams than flowers.

Lost among dreams,
I found a part of me
 while searching for you.

The best part of my dreams
are spent with you.

In everything I do,
 there is the whisper of you.

Soft pillows,
  unholy curves,
   crown splattered hair,
    sheets tangled,
     legs intertwined,
      forgotten dreams,

Pentecostal screams.

There's magic in her hips,
 and I want her
  to teach me all her tricks.

The greatest stories
 are those that we haven't lived yet.

Of all the past lives,
 I liked this one the best.

When she danced,
 she forgot everything,
except what it was like
to be a child again.

All your little flaws
 are what makes you perfect.

When she closes her eyes,
anything is possible.

Dream of me:

till you wake next to me again.

Foucault was lost in the madness
of humanity's cruelness.

We're all just Roy Batty...
Tears lost in the rain.

(The day Rutger Hauer died)

The continual self-gratification of
sharing your life with others isn't living.

"You don't actually believe people landed
on the moon,"
my grandmother once said to me.

Making me question everything
anyone had ever told me.

Between dreams and wishes,
we often discover the truth.

The voice I hear in my head
doesn't sound like me.

She dreamt of any life,
other than this one.

I like to pick up used books,
and read only the notes in the margins.

The immense distance between us,
only made the need to hold you greater.

Lost in thought,
because every one leads back to you.

Sometimes,
the loudest sound is silence.

Most parties are just excuses
to be alone around people.

Wittgenstein wouldn't like this:

Language is a cheating lover,
never telling the same story twice.

Love:

When you want to take all of
someone's pain,
and ask for nothing in return.

I want to bottle up
how I feel about you,
And send it to you to open
whenever you need to feel loved.

Wanting you every day,
feels like Orpheus
after looking back.

I want to wake up next to you.
Hand laying on my chest.
The warmth of your skin against mine.
Messy hair, sprawled everywhere.
The smell of you filling my every breathe.

Fragments from a dream:

Wisps of hair draped over her sleepy multi-
colored eyes.
Forcing my fingers to brush aside the strands
over and over,
floating in the soft whisper of a breeze.

Head in my lap,
starring into the very nature of me.

Tongue wetting the corners of dry lips.

Watching the slow rhythm of her chest rise
and fall.

Unwilling to disturb the slightest fabric of this
stillness.

Locked in this moment between each breath.
Wanting never to wake.

Math is the language
without a lover,

forever reducing the world to one.

Life:

And just like that it was over,
just as short as a childhood romance,
and just as unimportant.

Someone should collect all the forgotten
phrases displaced by technology:

The rabbit died.
Drop a dime.
Film at 11.
Don't touch that dial.
Roll up the window.

Forgotten within a century,
like most of us.

Stop living your whole life
preparing for tomorrow,
never realizing all the things you missed today.

Whenever I want to laugh,
I think of you standing there nude,
wearing a New Year's Eve hat,
giggling hysterically
while I snapped pictures of you.

They sat there,
 indifferent,
yet connected.

He knew her every movement,
without even watching her.

Maybe that's what love is,
  knowing the other person
without paying attention.

All these thoughts,
were lost in the chaos
between dreams and reality.